UNSUNG

Saumyah

BookLeaf
Publishing

India | USA | UK

UNSUNG © 2024 Saumyah

All rights reserved.

No part of this publication may be reproduced, stored in a retrieval system, or transmitted, in any form or by any means, electronic, mechanical, photocopying, recording or otherwise, without the prior written permission of the presenters.

Saumyah asserts the moral right to be identified as the author of this work.

Presentation by *BookLeaf Publishing*

Web: www.bookleafpub.com

E-mail: info@bookleafpub.com

ISBN: 9789363315082

First edition 2024

To my parents, Neelam and Shailendra, who have been my support forever. My Brother, who despite quarrelling with me on a daily basis, still is my best supporter. And to my friend Tarini, who's always told me to start publishing my books.

I thank you all.

ACKNOWLEDGEMENT

I would like to acknowledge the debt of extraordinary people who introduced me to so many emotions and feelings.

PREFACE

The intent of poems in this book is to let the reader interpret it as they wish. Yet I hope you face all your deep dark emotions and overcome them with a shine that compels you to fight against all odds, or enjoy what comes your way.

Before you start reading these poems though, I want to tell you that a lot of these poems were to never see the light, that's what I had decided, for I honestly believed that they aren't how contemporary poems are. It was just me playing with words and building on emotions, that I used to impress someone. I never thought I had it in me. Honestly, I still think I am dreaming. Publishing my own poetry book; you have to be joking, right?

But no it isn't, it is true. And this courage was bestowed upon me when I laid unconscious in the ICU ward of a hospital for four days. Those four days gave me the clarity that I needed to leave behind something of my own. To encourage people like me who struggle on an hourly basis to master the very art of broken bravery to fight everything that life throws at us.

TABLE OF CONTENTS

My Nymph

The grass was too green,
And the flowers too fond,
That sparkle in your eyes,
Sizzling fire by the pond,
Nobody knows and nobody saw,
It is a secret I hold, dear,
That you kissed me to stars.

The one with the white sail.

Afraid to call
Sitting by the waterfall,
Pouring my letters with breathings of heart,
Maybe I'll catch a cold or will I freeze again,

My sides shiver cold without you,
Flying to flickering flames beside you,
Wailing for light in a blinding tunnel,
Like a moth to roam by celestial compass cue.

I'll take all the risk on the six behind you.
This is crazy to miss, and too complex to tally,
We can climb the hills,
And ride the valleys,
A journey to the sea with the white sail,
To make it legal and stamp the licence.

A Delicate Dance of Intertwined Melodies

In realms of grace, where beauty resides,
A delicate dance, like whispers in the tides.
Ethereal beings, with steps so refined,
A symphony of motion, in perfect design.

These bodies, like feathers, light as the air,
They pirouette gently, without a care.
Every movement, a brushstroke of art,
A ballet of souls, where dreams impart.

With twirls and spins, she enchants the night,
Her elegance, a mesmerising sight.
Graceful as swans, in a moonlit trance,
We float and glide, in this delicate dance.

Each gesture, a story, untold and unseen,
Expressing emotions, with thy every routine.
Like petals in bloom, they blossom and sway,
A tapestry of emotions, woven in a ballet.

A delicate dance, a language unspoken,
Through leaps and bounds, hearts are awoken.
With every arabesque, we touch the divine,
A celestial rhythm, in motion so fine.

With every step, a story is told,
Of love and desire, oh so bold.
Gentle movements, like a feather's caress,
Igniting flames, a fiery duet.

Each movement, manifesting fire,
Burning brightly, such desires inspire.
They surrender to the music's sweet embrace,
A dance of passion, for a heavenly trace.

Autumn's Golden Symphony...

The golden leaves do rustle below,
As Autumn's whisper moves the trees to and fro.
Nature's song plays its melodic tune,
As Summer sings its fond adieu.

The trees in amber and scarlet dressed,
Their hues adorn in colours blessed.
The air is crisp with scents so fair,
A cosy warmth spreads everywhere.

On the wind's breath the message sings,
Of changes the coming season brings.
The birds rehearse their calls with care,
In Nature's orchestra beyond compare.

The sun paints the sky in shades so bright,
Of orange and red, a dazzling light.
A masterpiece of beauty is shown,
That leaves all in awe, in wonder thrown.

We know that Winter soon will come,
And leaves fade from branches tumble.
But let us cherish while we can,
This symphony of Autumn's grand plan.

The leaves' soft rustle-like music flows,
In Nature's eternal rhythm it goes.
A gentle reminder of her love,
That gives this gift from above.

So let us dance among the leaves aglow,
And sing along with the winds that blow,
For Autumn's symphony is a delight,
We should embrace with all our might.

Poem of the Past

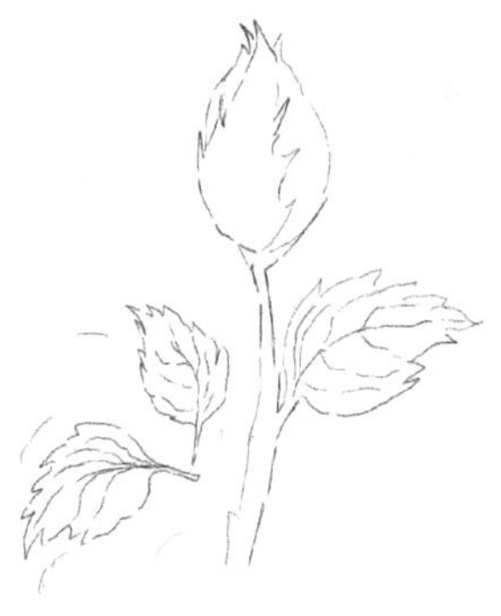

Rain fades in the falls,
As leaves whisper change,
The earth's rhythm calls,
For growth to rearrange.

The drops wash away,
The remnants of the vain,
Nature's gentle sway,
Invites us to reign.

The sound of the rain,
A lullaby to soul,
A reminder to refrain,
From holding onto the old.

These falls are a symbol,
Of seasons passing by,

Gently leaves crunch,
As time continues to fly.

It's time to shed,
The layers of the past,
And embrace instead,
The changes coming fast.

For like the rain,
We must fade and evolve,
In order to attain,
The beauty of resolve.

Persevere our growth,
And embrace the unknown,
For that is the oath,
Nature brightly has shown.

Rain fades in the falls,
But growth will always remain,
Presence divine asks to answer the call,
To ever keep growing, and never be the same.

A Railroad Rhyme

A book with tales untold waits to be penned,
Adventures on iron rails to far lands without
end.
Each journey brings renewal, a fresh start ever
new,
Through valleys and hillsides, vistas in view.

With eager soul and curious mind,
I steer this machine like no other kind.
The rails stretch far, challenges arise each day,
But memories sweet make toil worth the way.

'Tis now my time on these tracks to navigate,
My engine is ready each turn to negate.
A chance for myself and my spirit to know,
This ride is not simply my body's show.

Strangers I'll meet with stories to share,
Their lives interweave, as moments repair.
In others' eyes are glimpses of life I espy,
A world where as one our spirits fly high.

Each day on these rails are lessons abound,
Ever evolving, my being to compound.
With each whistle blow cares float on the breeze,
Dancing and whispering hope beneath dawn's
trees.

By the Window of
My Starry Muse!

With each fleeting glimmer of light overhead,
A story in my mind begins to spread.
Unknown visions in private musings told,
See the secrets that my dear heart holds?

Oh, wondrous night! The lone star's plight,
Sharing secrets in pale moonlight.
Deep in my soul it has always shone bright,
A beacon shining, a part of delight.

With every flicker, a tale enters my mind,
As secrets unveil by your window and some
dreams, I find.
You hear my message and see my sight,
Through lofty visions on a starry night.

A solitary star, in no book has its part,
Revolving alone to share its heart.
Compelling companions on adventures anew,
Where it guides our fate in skies ever blue.

Whispering a Thousand Stories

In a crowded room, our eyes did meet,
A fleeting moment, a glance so sweet.
Yet time itself stood frozen in place,
To thaw in a cosmic embrace.

These deceiving eyes of ours, in a gaze
profound,
A tale of longing told without a sound.
That single moment souls intertwined,
Erupts a universe where divinity shined.

A dance of desire, a fire that had burned within,
In that lingering glance, how hearts had yearned.

Oh how I wish that glance could last,
But alas, like sand it slipped from my hand,
Leaving an ache, a pining for eyes to withstand.
Yet that fluttering cannot grow cold.

Your eyes sometimes guide me on my journey's
way,
Like a beacon of hope in life's darkest days.
A moment where souls find deep connection,
Is a reminder of love's sweet infinite affection.

Unsung Symphony

O Beautiful one, though thy love eludes my
grasp,
Like a song lost to memory in life's strife,
Yet from sorrow's ashes shall I rise, reborn,
For within my soul burns passion's flame,
keeping me warm.

Each refrain and cry poured forth from my
heart's well,
Seeks to spread love's message that in song it
may dwell.
But will you ever see love shining through me?
Or am I but a tune unsung in this life's
symphony?

'Tis in music's hallowed realm I find solace and
peace,
Where echoing notes calm my troubled mind's
lease.
There upon the stage, sanctuary from worldly
woes,
Singing my heart for a love no one knows.

In life's tale, my part is the loudest I shall play,
With guitars roaring and heartbeat carrying the
day.
And even without thy love which my soul doth
crave,
Through this music, my spirit brave shall
evermore wave.

Courage Commands to Dive Deep

On a trail to a cold mountain!
Is a walk to the ancient post office!
Emulating Baltic the fountains had cried,
But courage shall prevail over winter tide.

Perhaps your hatch may suffer a chill,
Some paths make even the bravest ill.
But adventure calls from valley's winding way,
Have faith, my friend, as to the Lord we pray!

The frost-capped peaks commands explorer's
feet,
What mysteries in nature's folds we'll meet.
So, bundle up warm against the breeze's bite,
On this wintry path, to find passion and delight!

Nature's gifts are yours to claim,
Fly to the mountains by the flickering flames,
Hold the lamps or bask in their burn,
For silver light shines when the choo-choo train
comes.

Hey Moon

Hey moon,
Walk with me tonight,
As I long for you,
Let me break the clock,
For me and you.

Dear super-moon,
Break the rules tonight,
As I talk to you,
Let me share my heat,
For a slice of you.

My beautiful blue moon,
Shine for me tonight,
As I sway for you,
Let me touch your rays,
Shining purple and blue,

Oh lovely crescent moon,
Sleep with me tonight,
As I sing to you,
Let me hold your hands,
Let me hold you close.

My rushing blood moon,
Breathe with me tonight,
As I lean on you,
Are you wild for me?
As I am wild for you.

Such shivers, oh dear white moon,
Let me steal you for tonight,
As I reach for you,
Let me kiss your lips,
Soft and slow.

The Dangerous Attire

Leave that up to me,
Let me show you how it's meant to be.
Scroll it, roll it, hold it free,
Bite into the open sea.

My love, come lay with me,
Let our passions run freely.
Our hearts and souls forever entwine,
In a dance that's sung as old as time.

Our hands explore with care and zest,
As our lips meet with love professed.
Skin to skin our bodies meld,
In each other's arms we're held.

Lost in waves of pure delight,
Under moon and stars so bright.
Time stands still yet races fast,
This moment of bliss will ever last.

Leave that up to me,
Let me show you how it rolls.
We'll trade and pop and play,
Like a bomb that's dropped and blows.

The game of who gets is hot,
The desire to tame a fire,
And the smiles of dame and one,
The one that had dangerous attire.

My darling one, my heart's desire,
Now we fan the lover's flame higher and higher.
In your sweet embrace so kind,
All I've hoped and prayed to find.

The One With Power

The stony hands, ring the clock!
Sitting by the moon's stark!
Just because, just because,
He's the boss, and I'm the horse.

Favour the one with a fine black flout cloak,
Nobs and Toffs that despise those he openly
disregards,
Transient gratification of that rich block,
Upright mighty feathers, together they flock.

Humming the tumbledown hymns of,
Old McDonald's Diggory dock,
Seizing their ounce for his fat stock.

Just because just because,
He's the boss, and I'm the horse.

Ping Pong Games!

Maybe it was the monsoon breeze,
That had me so at ease,
You were just a classmate then,
Neither was I up for seize,
Then you called my name,
and we played a ping pong game,
I had happiness in my eyes,
filled with fluttering butterflies.
I smiled a little when you laughed a lot,
we lost the game but,
Gained two hearts.

It stirred me boldly once again,
when you carelessly held my hand,
That day we had locked a stare,
Like the ones, we never shared,
Silence hadn't been in my plan,
but that twinkling night had a golden dawn.
Your friends have started to ship our names,

They say when it comes, we can't budge,
What's the game here?
Wherever I'd go you are always there,
Like you are waiting for me,
Waiting for my care

Even by the stables, standing by the mare,
'twas the second time, we had locked a long
stare,
My feet had dared when I walked to you,
Like my heart had stopped, but so did you,
You covered it well and I had to take the cue.

You surely were a player,
By October, you had a new girl,
I was a burned-out candle as you smiled with
her,
Looking back on those days,
Both of us had made many mistakes.
when the wind had whistled on your hair,
we once again had locked a stare,
But I didn't look up, I couldn't dare
I asked myself "Why the long grudge?"
like a painted pot with a bitter-looking glaze,
Even fate has a frown now on his face.
A losing game of slot, women beware!
'Cause the higher it goes,
the deeper it sunk.

It was the end of December now,
My heart was beating hard for a hinge,
Such a pity, for we had what it took,
But would be unsung, my fondness for you.
By the rhythm of the storm my soul pled to you,
You had covered it well and I had to take the
cue.

Fading Echoes of Fondness

In shadows so dim, alone do I stand,
A lone silhouette in this crowded land.
Like a tune forgot at night's dark end,
Lost in the void, from a barren sight I rend.

O'er and o'er the love meets its fall,
Yet my defiant heart for thee stands tall.
Thou turn away, sees not at all,
The wounds deep thy indifference enthrals.

Easily passed o'er by my life's delight,
Like a song forgotten in strife's plight.
A Phoenix from ashes shall I rise anew,
My spirit's grand fire still burns true.

Strings of devotion played mighty just,
But deaf are thine ears to my heart's thrust.
With hope swelling sought to part the veil,
Yet goes unsung my love's fond tale.

O'er and o'er have I sung for thy fondness,
Alas, thee dances but to thine own fair chances.
In this ballad of void, I am a lone figure to be,
Strumming my soul, dancing with a heart left to
wither and flee.

Sing a Song Instead

Raging at my Carol, my heart feels so heavy,
Words left unsaid, emotions unsteady,
Why did she hurt me, what did I do wrong,
Maybe I talk too much instead of singing a song.

But for now, I'll sit with my anger and pain,
And try to understand what fuelled this flame,
Perhaps with time and space, we can make
things right,
And find a way to love and hold each other tight.

A Love That Wouldn't
Stand the Perish

Rammed to know what's really goin' on,
These mysteries got me scratchin' my stone.
Things seem a mess up in here,
These empty scales just ain't got nothin' to fear.

This warm fuzzy feelin' ain't mine to enjoy,
This lovin' just wouldn't last, it was doomed to
destroy.
This relationship swung like pendulums do,
Now it's all burnt up, just look at the view!

Child is to get to the bottom of things said my
pastor,
These thoughts are to be locked behind a
boulder even faster.
Inside's a wreck, a total disaster,
These scales got nothin' to weigh, where's that
blaster!

This cosy warmth wasn't for me to have and to
hold,
This lovin' just wouldn't take me to grow old.
Back and forth did this romance sway,
Leavin' scorched what used to stay.

Story of a Car Ride
and Its Tears

Amidst the whispers of a soul set free,
Rose a chaos of heart's stormy tree.
It demands of tears caressing sorrow's hand,
Embracing the wound as waves upon the sand.

It is not because they don't care,
Rather a soul that has much fear.
Within these shadows, fear does reside,
A tender heart with scars to hide.

A closet full and an empty heart,
Confused to tell light and darkness apart.
A fragile soul, that's burned before,
Will tremble to knock at love's open door.

'Twas not for lack of care that tears did fall,
But fear by then had held heart in its thrall.
Deep in shadows dark, terror held its place,
As scars upon spirit, I tried to erase.

I still have the jar that's filled with pain,
Forever craving, and forever in vain
A fragile soul by flames seared and torn,
At love's door now dared I drawl and mourn.

Not My Guy!

Oh boy, do I ever want to uncover the mysteries,
buried in that rocky heart of his!
There have got to be many secrets locked away
in his heart, un-discovered.
His emotions for her deep inside are obvious
when his voice trembles,
Even if he tries to keep the scales outside all
balanced or jumbled.

I would have loved to cherish that warmth,
and lay in the tenderness he sometimes showed,
If only he had let me in instead of blaming me
away.
A love really tested against time, was washed
away.

Emotions swelling at the rate of a dime.
This love really ran against the time.
Now all that's left is ashes and soot,
Where my happiness forever did stand its roots.

You may have fortune, if I get to see the hidden
and unspoken shut behind,
A guy like him has demons in his depths.
Listen and you can feel the turmoil raging
inside,
Even now, on the world stage, he rages as his
pretentious acts fail to paint him kind.

A woman won't show, but she would always
know.
That heat and that passion was hers to hold.
For years, she had feared, if he'd ever more
commit,
But affection for him has been fleeting bit by bit.

Unspoken

A warmth that wasn't mine to cherish,
A risible scheme of hearts.
Slaved to the way you swayed,
Relishing the fine work of Gods.

The warmth of your embrace I could never own,
Our hearts danced to a tune not our own,
Enslaved puppy to your graceful moves,
Finding solace in the heavens above.

Deep isn't what's in shambles within,
A fair trade to judge me more.
Mysteries of a cold heart,
Don't I know what's unspoken for...

Alas, my heart hath been warmed by another flame,
Since thy scheming ways did tear my soul.
Enslaved was I to your charms and sway,
In thine eyes I saw visions of reality above all.

It is a chasm wider than even the mind can plumb.
As if one could assess the madness of another.
What riddles do you present in your aloof land?
When substance slips like desert sand.

The turmoil within my soul cannot be seen,
To assess me further is an unfair scheme,
The enigma of your icy heart remains,
That which remains unsaid, says I remain.

Rain Drops Passin' By

Raindrops be pitter pattin' on the waterfall
cascade,
Leaves they be whisperin' "make way for
change, don't be afraid."
Earth just groovin' to nature's funky beat,
Things'll rearrange, however, they want, ain't
nothing more sweet!

The drops wash away what's old and passed,
Nature digs her mellow vibe so it's sure to last.
The sound of rain, a soul's lullaby,
Chill out and remember days gone by.

That waterfall, symbolizin' seasons come and
go,
Leaves in the breeze got a message you need to
know.

This rain will wash away what came before,
For tomorrow through open doors we'll explore.
Nurture our growth and roll with the flow,
'Cause Nature always teaches the resolute she
knows.

"My Dearest Moon"
(A Hey Moon Alternate Version)

My Dearest Moon,

Walk by my side this night,
For I have been longing for your light.
Let me steal this time, just you and me,
Under starry skies, for our hearts to be free.

Break the rules with me, my love,
As we talk for a night of what lies above.
Let me bask in your soothing glow,
Touch a slice of heaven, as I leave for the war.

Shine down on me, my radiant moon,
As in your beams, I sway and swoon.
Let me again feel your soft caress,
Purple and blue, your loveliness.

Sleep with me tonight, oh my moon so fair,
I will sing you songs of love on the midnight air.
Let me hold you close 'til the dawn's first light,
In your shining embrace, throughout the long
night.

Steal this moment, my moonlight dear,
As I reach out to you, with my heart so sincere.
Let me kiss your sweet lips, soft and slow,
Under these star-spangled skies, our love aglow.

Now the morning sun awakens me to a new day,
As the night gives way to light, and my moon
slips away.
Though clouds may come between us and miles
may keep us apart,
You remain in my soul and hold the key to my
heart.

The one with warmth and winter.

Sun setting on the horizon,
Filling hearts like the city of Brighton,
Colours bright,
Pure delight,

Streets are singing like a cukcoo,
Bidding the sunset's warm golden hue,
With feelings, that are pure and true,
For love, the sky is forever blue.

Stirring up the heart, a sunset can,
The moon comes up, but lovers can't,
But the beauty still blooms,
Hope fills up rooms.

But the squaddies are keeping up the fight,
Captain's orders for everyone to rest the sight,
Pivot! Pivot! On a cold winter night,
Close your eyes and snuggle up tight.

www.ingramcontent.com/pod-product-compliance
Lightning Source LLC
La Vergne TN
LVHW021255200726
843509LV00012B/1674